TÖILETRIVIA™

BASEBALL

The only trivia book that caters to your everyday bathroom needs

by Jeremy Klaff & Harry Klaff

This book might contain product names, trademarks, or registered trademarks. All trademarks in this book are property of their respective owners. If used, they are for non-biased use, and we do not encourage or discourage use of said product or service. Any term suspected of being a trademark will be properly capitalized.

Cover art by Stephanie Strack

About the Authors

Harry Klaff covered the NHL for *The Hockey News* and *Hockey Pictorial*, and reported for both the Associated Press and United Press International. He has written three books, *All Time Greatest Super Bowl*, *All Time Greatest Stanley Cup*, and *Computer Literacy and Use.*

Today, he is a retired Social Studies teacher from Brooklyn. Because he never went on a date in his adolescence, Harry had plenty of time to research useless facts and figures on everything ranging from history to pop culture. Moonlighting as a hockey scoreboard operator and baseball beer vendor, Harry had ample time to collect data.

Yet somehow, he got married. In 1977, Jeremy was born. Rather than being raised on a steady diet of carrots and peas, baby Jeremy was forced to learn facts from textbooks. His first word was "Uzbekistan." Throughout his childhood, Jeremy had a hard time making friends. When other kids wanted to play baseball, he wanted to instruct them about Henry VIII's six wives. After a failed career as a standup comic and broadcaster, in 2000 Jeremy fittingly became a Social Studies teacher. Today he brings trivia to the next generation.

Collect All Toiletrivia Titles

US History

World History

Pop Culture

Sports

Baseball

Music

and more!

Get the full list of titles at
www.toiletrivia.com

Acknowledgements

We at Toiletrivia would like to thank all of the people who made this possible.

- The ancient cities of Harappa and Mohenjo Daro for engineering advances in plumbing.
- Sir John Harrington for inventing the modern flush toilet.
- Seth Wheeler for his patent of perforated toilet paper.
- Jeffrey Gunderson for inventing the plunger.

We would like to thank our families for suffering through nights of endless trivia.

We would also like to thank the friendly commuters at the Grand Central Station restroom facility for field testing these editions.

Introduction

Here at *Toiletrivia* we do extensive research on what you, the bathroom user, wish to see in your reading material. Sure, there are plenty of fine books out there to pass the time, but none of them cater to your competitive needs. That's why *Toiletrivia* is here to provide captivating trivia that allows you to interact with fellow bathroom users.

Each chapter allows you to keep score so you can evaluate your progress if you choose to go through the book multiple times. Or, you may wish to leave the book behind for others to play and keep score against you. Perhaps you just want to make it look like you are a genius, and leave a perfect scorecard for all to see. We hope you leave one in every bathroom of the house.

The rules of *Toiletrivia* are simple. Each chapter has 30 questions divided into three sections…One Roll, Two Rolls, or Three Rolls. The One Rolls are easiest and worth one point. Two Rolls are a bit harder and are worth two points. And of course, Three Rolls are the hardest, and are worth three points. You will tabulate your progress on the scorecard near the end of the book.

The questions we have selected are meant for dinner conversation, or impressing people you want to date. With few exceptions, our queries are geared for the uncomfortable situations that life throws at you, like when you have nothing in common with someone, and need to offer some clever banter. We hope that the facts you learn in the restroom make it easier to meet your future in-laws, or deal with that hairdresser who just won't stop talking to you.

Remember, *Toiletrivia* is a game. No joysticks, no computer keyboards…just you, your toilet, and a pen; the way nature intended it. So good luck. We hope you are triumphant.

DIRECTIONS

Each set of questions has an answer sheet opposite it. Write your answers in the first available column to the right. When you are done with a set of 10 questions, ***fold*** your answer column underneath so the next restroom user doesn't see your answers. *Special note to restroom users 2 and 3: No cheating! And the previous person's answers might be wrong!*

Then check your responses with the answer key in the back of the book. Mark your right answers with a check, and your wrong answers with an "x." Then go to the scorecard on pages 98-100 and tabulate your results. These totals will be the standard for other users to compare.

Be sure to look online for other Toiletrivia titles
Visit us at www.toiletrivia.com

Table of Contents

Great Moments

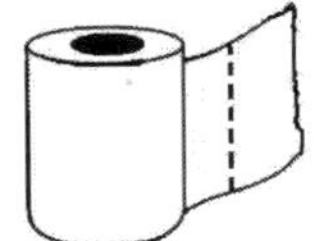

One Roll

1. Why were all baseball fans' eyes on Fulton County Stadium April 8, 1974?

2. Who pitched the only no-hit game in a Division Series on Oct. 6, 2010?

3. What did Roger Clemens do for the second time on Sept. 18, 1996?

4. What highlight of Nolan Ryan's career was recorded against Toronto on May 1, 1991?

5. Who struck out 19 Padres, including the last 10 in a row, at Shea Stadium on April 22, 1970?

6. What record did Bob Gibson set on Oct. 2, 1968 against the Detroit Tigers?

7. Who fired the only perfect game in World Series history on Oct. 8, 1956?

8. On May 30, 1956, his majestic blast off the façade just missed being the first home run hit out of Yankee Stadium.

9. Whose homer in the bottom of the 9th inning of Game 6 off of Mitch Williams gave the Toronto Blue Jays the 1993 World Series?

10. Red Sox pitcher Tracy Stallard gave up a memorable home run on Oct. 1, 1961. Who hit it?

Answer Sheet **Great Moments** **1 Roll**	**Answer Sheet** **Great Moments** **1 Roll**	**Answer Sheet** **Great Moments** **1 Roll**
Name________________	**Name**________________	**Name**________________
1.	1.	1.
2.	2.	2.
3.	3.	3.
4.	4.	4.
5.	5.	5.
6.	6.	6.
7.	7.	7.
8.	8.	8.
9.	9.	9.
10.	10.	10.

After you have filled out the sheet, fold your column underneath along the dashed line so the next restroom user won't see your answers. ***The first player uses the far right column.***

Notes:	***Notes:***	***Notes:***

Great Moments

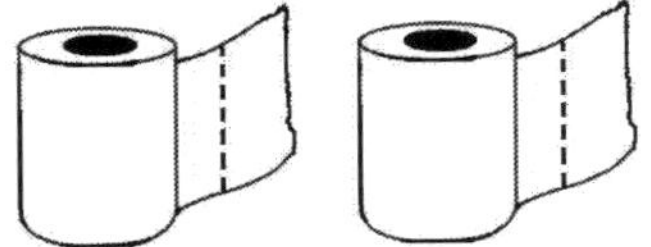

Two Rolls

1. What couldn't Jack Buck believe what he just saw on Oct. 15, 1988?

2. On Sept. 14, 1968, this Detroit Tigers righthander became the last pitcher to win 30 games in a season.

3. Whose home run in the bottom of the 9th inning of Game 7 enabled the Pirates to beat the Yankees in the 1960 World Series?

4. Why was the first night game at Wrigley Field really *not* the first night game at Wrigley Field?

5. What team won the 7th game of the 1991 World Series 1-0 with a run in the bottom of the 10th inning?

6. Whose home run in the 12th inning of Game 4 of the 2004 ALCS started Boston's remarkable comeback from a 3-0 deficit in games against the Yankees?

7. How did Ted Williams conclude his career on Sept. 28, 1960?

8. How was history made at the first night game ever at Ebbets Field on June 15, 1938?

9. What N.Y. Giants ace struck out five future American League Hall of Famers in a row in the 1934 All-Star Game?

10. Why did Joe DiMaggio have a bad day in Cleveland on July 17, 1941?

Answer Sheet	Answer Sheet	Answer Sheet
Great Moments 2 Rolls	Great Moments 2 Rolls	Great Moments 2 Rolls
Name__________	Name__________	Name__________
1.	1.	1.
2.	2.	2.
3.	3.	3.
4.	4.	4.
5.	5.	5.
6.	6.	6.
7.	7.	7.
8.	8.	8.
9.	9.	9.
10.	10.	10.

After you have filled out the sheet, fold your column underneath along the dashed line so the next restroom user won't see your answers. ***The first player uses the far right column.***

Notes:	*Notes:*	*Notes:*

Great Moments

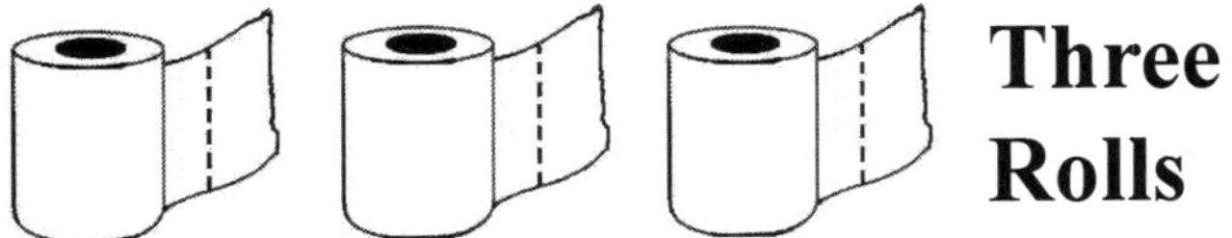

Three Rolls

1. Who hit the only grand slam home run in All-Star Game history?

2. On May 1, 1920, Brooklyn's Leon Cadore and Boston's Joe Oeschger pitched complete games. What was so special?

3. In Game 3 of the 1969 World Series, what N.Y. Mets outfielder drove in 5 runs and saved 5 runs with his glove?

4. Who served up Carlton Fisk's 12th inning home run in Game 6 of the 1975 World Series?

5. On Aug. 15, 1926, three Brooklyn Dodgers wound up on third base at the same time. How did it happen? (Players' names are not required.)

6. What San Diego Padres pitcher gave up Pete Rose's 4,192nd career hit to pass Ty Cobb on Sept. 11, 1985?

7. Who made a mad dash to score from first base in Game 7 of the 1946 World Series while Johnny Pesky "snoozed?"

8. On Sept. 23, 1908, a N.Y. Giant rookie committed "Merkle's Boner" against the Chicago Cubs. What did he do?

9. What was 1938's famous "Homer in the Gloamin'"?

10. What did pitchers Hippo Vaughn of the Cubs and Fred Toney of the Reds both do on May 2, 1917?

Answer Sheet Great Moments 3 Rolls Name________________	**Answer Sheet** Great Moments 3 Rolls Name________________	**Answer Sheet** Great Moments 3 Rolls Name________________
1.	1.	1.
2.	2.	2.
3.	3.	3.
4.	4.	4.
5.	5.	5.
6.	6.	6.
7.	7.	7.
8.	8.	8.
9.	9.	9.
10.	10.	10.

After you have filled out the sheet, fold your column underneath along the dashed line so the next restroom user won't see your answers. ***The first player uses the far right column.***

Notes:	***Notes:***	***Notes:***

Ballparks

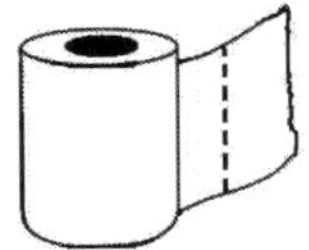

One Roll

1. Where did the Los Angeles Dodgers play when they first moved to California?

2. Where did the Pittsburgh Pirates play between 1909 and 1970?

3. What modern ballpark has a large warehouse beyond the right field fence with lights atop?

4. What was the first domed stadium used by a Major League team?

5. What is green, about 39 feet high, and has people sitting on top of it?

6. In the movie *A League of Their Own*, in what real ballpark were the tryouts held?

7. Where did the Philadelphia Phillies play from 1971 until 2003?

8. In what city do kayakers fight for home run balls?

9. Where did President George W. Bush throw out a ceremonial first pitch shortly after 9/11?

10. Mark Grace was the first to splash a home run into this ballpark's swimming pool.

Answer Sheet	Answer Sheet	Answer Sheet
Ballparks **1 Roll**	**Ballparks** **1 Roll**	**Ballparks** **1 Roll**
Name________________	**Name**________________	**Name**________________
1.	1.	1.
2.	2.	2.
3.	3.	3.
4.	4.	4.
5.	5.	5.
6.	6.	6.
7.	7.	7.
8.	8.	8.
9.	9.	9.
10.	10.	10.

After you have filled out the sheet, fold your column underneath along the dashed line so the next restroom user won't see your answers. ***The first player uses the far right column.***

Notes: | ***Notes:*** | ***Notes:***

Ballparks

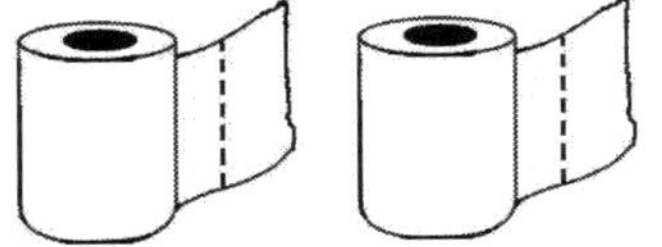

Two Rolls

1. Why is only one of the rows at Coors Field a different color (purple)?

2. What ballpark was situated on Coogan's Bluff?

3. What modern ballpark was originally sponsored by a company that infamously went bankrupt?

4. What was Tiger Stadium called between 1938 and 1960?

5. What ballpark saw exploding disco records?

6. In what ballpark did Roseanne Barr sing her "rendition" of the National Anthem?

7. After Fenway Park and Wrigley Field, what is currently the oldest ballpark in MLB?

8. What ballpark featured a sign that said "Hit Sign, Win Suit" at the bottom of the scoreboard?

9. In what ballpark did the Beatles perform in 1965 and 1966?

10. What ballpark currently in use was the first to have a retractable roof?

Answer Sheet **Ballparks** **2 Rolls** **Name**________________	**Answer Sheet** **Ballparks** **2 Rolls** **Name**________________	**Answer Sheet** **Ballparks** **2 Rolls** **Name**________________
1.	1.	1.
2.	2.	2.
3.	3.	3.
4.	4.	4.
5.	5.	5.
6.	6.	6.
7.	7.	7.
8.	8.	8.
9.	9.	9.
10.	10.	10.

After you have filled out the sheet, fold your column underneath along the dashed line so the next restroom user won't see your answers. ***The first player uses the far right column.***

Notes:	***Notes:***	***Notes:***

Ballparks

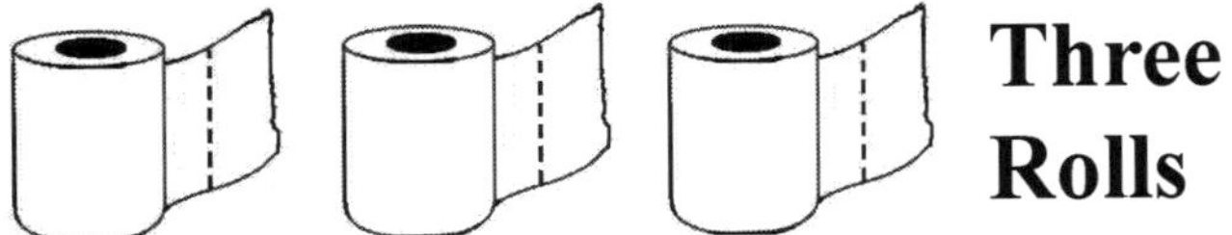

Three Rolls

1. Where did the Yankees play before moving to Yankee Stadium in 1923?

2. What ballpark of the past was often visited by US Presidents?

3. In 1914, for whom was Wrigley Field originally built? (It wasn't the Cubs. And it wasn't called Wrigley Field!)

4. What ballpark replaced Cleveland's "Mistake on the Lake" in 1994?

5. What is the name of the mascot who slides down after a Brewers home run at Miller Park?

6. What are the three rivers of old Three Rivers Stadium in Pittsburgh?

7. In the late 1940s and 1950s, the Pirates shortened their left field fence to accommodate two right-handed power hitters. What was either the "Gardens" or the "Korner" called?

8. What ballpark that was in use from 1912-1970 featured an incline in front of the fences instead of a warning track?

9. What was the first home of the Montreal Expos?

10. What was the original name of the first Busch Stadium in St. Louis?

Answer Sheet	Answer Sheet	Answer Sheet
Ballparks **3 Rolls**	**Ballparks** **3 Rolls**	**Ballparks** **3 Rolls**
Name______________	**Name**______________	**Name**______________
1.	1.	1.
2.	2.	2.
3.	3.	3.
4.	4.	4.
5.	5.	5.
6.	6.	6.
7.	7.	7.
8.	8.	8.
9.	9.	9.
10.	10.	10.

After you have filled out the sheet, fold your column underneath along the dashed line so the next restroom user won't see your answers. ***The first player uses the far right column.***

Notes:	***Notes:***	***Notes:***

Hitters

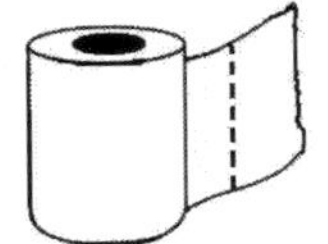

One Roll

1. What does "cleanup hitter" mean?

2. Who hit the most leadoff home runs?

3. What team's lineup was known as Murderers' Row?

4. What does it mean when a player "hits for the cycle?"

5. This player reached exactly 3,000 career hits just before he was tragically killed in a plane crash.

6. "Mr. October" was also "Mr. Whiff." He struck out the most times in a Major League career. Name him.

7. Who won the Most Valuable Player Award an incredible seven times?

8. What is the "wheelhouse?"

9. On Aug. 20, 1938, he hit his 23rd—and final—grand slam home run, adding to the record which he held on his own until Alex Rodriguez tied him in 2012.

10. What does it mean when a batter is "in the hole?"

Answer Sheet	Answer Sheet	Answer Sheet
Hitters **1 Roll**	**Hitters** **1 Roll**	**Hitters** **1 Roll**
Name________________	**Name**________________	**Name**________________
1.	1.	1.
2.	2.	2.
3.	3.	3.
4.	4.	4.
5.	5.	5.
6.	6.	6.
7.	7.	7.
8.	8.	8.
9.	9.	9.
10.	10.	10.

After you have filled out the sheet, fold your column underneath along the dashed line so the next restroom user won't see your answers. ***The first player uses the far right column.***

Notes:	***Notes:***	***Notes:***

Hitters

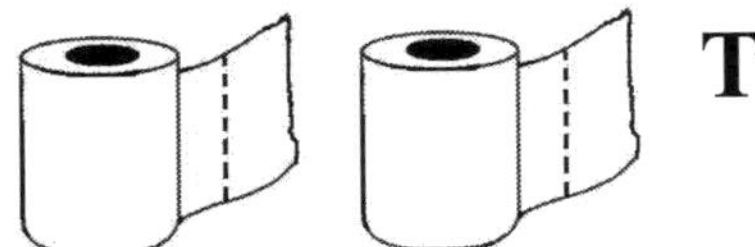

Two Rolls

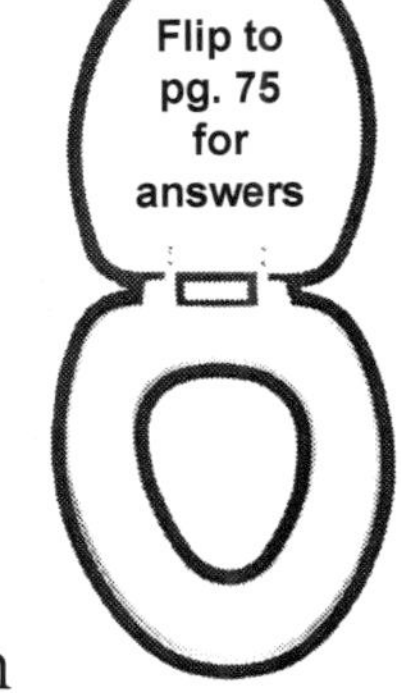

1. Who rank 1-2-3 in career batting average?

2. When Rickey Henderson stole his 939th base, whose record did he break?

3. Within six inches, what is the length and width of the batter's box?

4. You make the call. A batter swings and misses at a ball that hits him in the foot. What happens?

5. Two catchers have won the Most Valuable Player Award three times. Who are they?

6. No hitter wants to be saddled with the "Golden Sombrero." What is it?

7. Between Babe Ruth's 60 home runs in 1927, and Roger Maris' 61 home runs in 1961, two American Leaguers hit 58 homers in a season. Name one of them.

8. Cal Ripken played in 2,632 consecutive games. What was the magic number set by Lou Gehrig that he eclipsed?

9. Until Miguel Cabrera turned the trick in 2012, who was the last player to win the Triple Crown?

10. Modern maple bats seem to shatter often. What wood are more traditional bats made of?

Answer Sheet

Hitters
2 Rolls

Name__________________

1.
2.
3.
4.
5.
6.
7.
8.
9.
10.

Answer Sheet

Hitters
2 Rolls

Name__________________

1.
2.
3.
4.
5.
6.
7.
8.
9.
10.

Answer Sheet

Hitters
2 Rolls

Name__________________

1.
2.
3.
4.
5.
6.
7.
8.
9.
10.

After you have filled out the sheet, fold your column underneath along the dashed line so the next restroom user won't see your answers. ***The first player uses the far right column.***

Notes:

Notes:

Notes:

Hitters

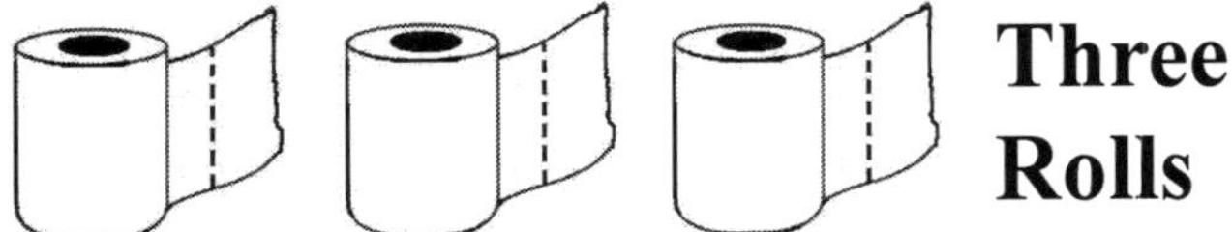

Three Rolls

1. Cal Ripken is the all time leader in a category that he wishes he wasn't. What is the category?

2. Five players with over 500 lifetime home runs have 4 or fewer letters in their last name. Name three of them.

3. Who has the highest lifetime batting average for a player who played after 1970?

4. This Houston Astro got hit with 285 pitches, the most in the modern era. Who is he?

5. There are four members of the 40-40 club (40 home runs and 40 stolen bases in a season). Name two.

6. Since Ted Williams hit .406 in 1941, what player has come the closest?

7. In 2003, this Atlanta Braves catcher set a record for most home runs by a backstop in a season with 42.

8. Why were batting averages ridiculously high back in 1887?

9. On Sept. 16, 1975, Pirate Rennie Stennett had a record hitting performance. What did he do?

10. Two players have won the Triple Crown twice. Name one of them.

Answer Sheet	Answer Sheet	Answer Sheet
Hitters 3 Rolls	Hitters 3 Rolls	Hitters 3 Rolls
Name________________	Name________________	Name________________
1.	1.	1.
2.	2.	2.
3.	3.	3.
4.	4.	4.
5.	5.	5.
6.	6.	6.
7.	7.	7.
8.	8.	8.
9.	9.	9.
10.	10.	10.

After you have filled out the sheet, fold your column underneath along the dashed line so the next restroom user won't see your answers. ***The first player uses the far right column.***

Notes:

Notes:

Notes:

Nicknames

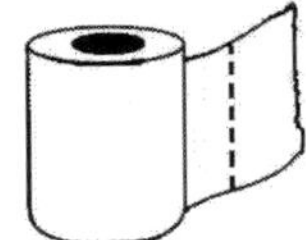

One Roll

1. The Bambino
2. Charlie Hustle
3. Joltin' Joe
4. A-Rod
5. Satchel
6. Hammerin' Hank
7. King Felix
8. Pee Wee
9. Big Papi
10. The Georgia Peach

Answer Sheet

Nicknames
1 Roll

Name________________

1.
2.
3.
4.
5.
6.
7.
8.
9.
10.

Answer Sheet

Nicknames
1 Roll

Name________________

1.
2.
3.
4.
5.
6.
7.
8.
9.
10.

Answer Sheet

Nicknames
1 Roll

Name________________

1.
2.
3.
4.
5.
6.
7.
8.
9.
10.

After you have filled out the sheet, fold your column underneath along the dashed line so the next restroom user won't see your answers. ***The first player uses the far right column.***

Notes:

Notes:

Notes:

Nicknames

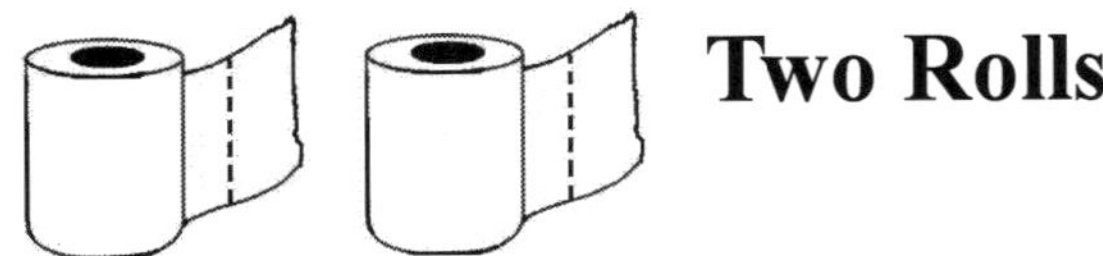

Two Rolls

Flip to pg. 78 for answers

1. Killer
2. Pudge
3. Wizard of Oz
4. The Old "Perfesser"
5. The Duke of Flatbush
6. The Scooter
7. K-Rod
8. Doctor K
9. The Splendid Splinter
10. Mr. Cub

Answer Sheet	Answer Sheet	Answer Sheet
Nicknames 2 Rolls	Nicknames 2 Rolls	Nicknames 2 Rolls
Name________________	Name________________	Name________________
1.	1.	1.
2.	2.	2.
3.	3.	3.
4.	4.	4.
5.	5.	5.
6.	6.	6.
7.	7.	7.
8.	8.	8.
9.	9.	9.
10.	10.	10.

After you have filled out the sheet, fold your column underneath along the dashed line so the next restroom user won't see your answers. ***The first player uses the far right column.***

Notes:	***Notes:***	***Notes:***

Nicknames

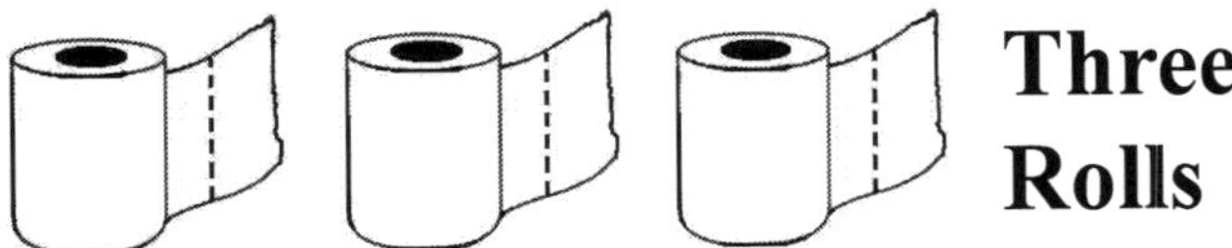

Flip to pg. 79 for answers

1. Ducky Wucky
2. Country
3. The Dominican Dandy
4. The Big Train
5. Big Six
6. Cool Papa
7. The Fordham Flash
8. Pepper
9. Pie
10. Rapid Robert

Answer Sheet **Nicknames** **3 Rolls**	**Answer Sheet** **Nicknames** **3 Rolls**	**Answer Sheet** **Nicknames** **3 Rolls**
Name________________	**Name**________________	**Name**________________
1.	1.	1.
2.	2.	2.
3.	3.	3.
4.	4.	4.
5.	5.	5.
6.	6.	6.
7.	7.	7.
8.	8.	8.
9.	9.	9.
10.	10.	10.

After you have filled out the sheet, fold your column underneath along the dashed line so the next restroom user won't see your answers. ***The first player uses the far right column.***

Notes:	***Notes:***	***Notes:***

Teams & Leagues

Flip to pg. 80 for answers

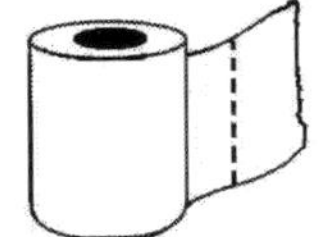

One Roll

1. What great team of the 1930s was nicknamed “The Gashouse Gang”?

2. Connie Mack managed this team for 50 years.

3. Who were the Black Sox?

4. What was the original name of the Houston Astros?

5. What team name originated from people scurrying out of the way of trolleys?

6. What was the first Major League franchise located outside of the United States?

7. What team moved to Minnesota in 1961 and became the Twins?

8. What team did Robert Redford’s Roy Hobbs play for in the 1984 film, *The Natural*?

9. This team made its debut in 1993 along with the Florida Marlins.

10. This 1982 team which led the AL in home runs was called “Harvey’s Wallbangers” after their manager, Harvey Kuenn. The team switched leagues in 1998. Who are they?

Answer Sheet	Answer Sheet	Answer Sheet
Teams & Leagues **1 Roll**	**Teams & Leagues** **1 Roll**	**Teams & Leagues** **1 Roll**
Name________________	**Name**________________	**Name**________________
1.	1.	1.
2.	2.	2.
3.	3.	3.
4.	4.	4.
5.	5.	5.
6.	6.	6.
7.	7.	7.
8.	8.	8.
9.	9.	9.
10.	10.	10.

After you have filled out the sheet, fold your column underneath along the dashed line so the next restroom user won't see your answers. ***The first player uses the far right column.***

Notes: ***Notes:*** ***Notes:***

Teams & Leagues

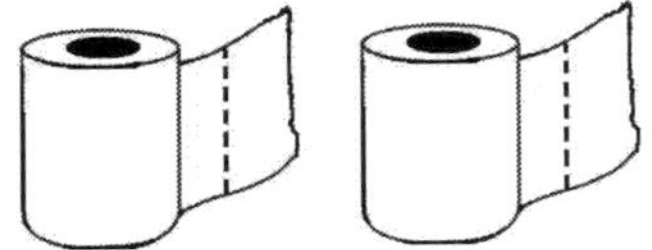

Two Rolls

1. On August 8, 1976, this team actually wore short pants.

2. What modern team won the World Series in only their fourth season?

3. What team was Bud Abbott the manager of in the famous comedy skit, *Who's on First*?

4. What was the name of Seattle's first Major League team in 1969?

5. What team moved from its original city in 1954 and became the Baltimore Orioles?

6. What city's pennant chances took a downturn when Mrs. O'Leary's cow kicked over a lamp?

7. Although not related to a modern-day franchise of the same name, this *amazing* team won its league's championship in 1884.

8. What was the N.Y. AL team known as before they were called Yankees?

9. What downtrodden team of the 1920s was affectionately known as "The Daffiness Boys?"

10. After playing in the same northeastern city from 1871 to 1952, this team moved to Milwaukee in 1953.

Answer Sheet	**Answer Sheet**	**Answer Sheet**
Teams & Leagues **2 Rolls**	**Teams & Leagues** **2 Rolls**	**Teams & Leagues** **2 Rolls**
Name________________	**Name**________________	**Name**________________
1.	1.	1.
2.	2.	2.
3.	3.	3.
4.	4.	4.
5.	5.	5.
6.	6.	6.
7.	7.	7.
8.	8.	8.
9.	9.	9.
10.	10.	10.

After you have filled out the sheet, fold your column underneath along the dashed line so the next restroom user won't see your answers. ***The first player uses the far right column.***

Notes:	***Notes:***	***Notes:***

Teams & Leagues

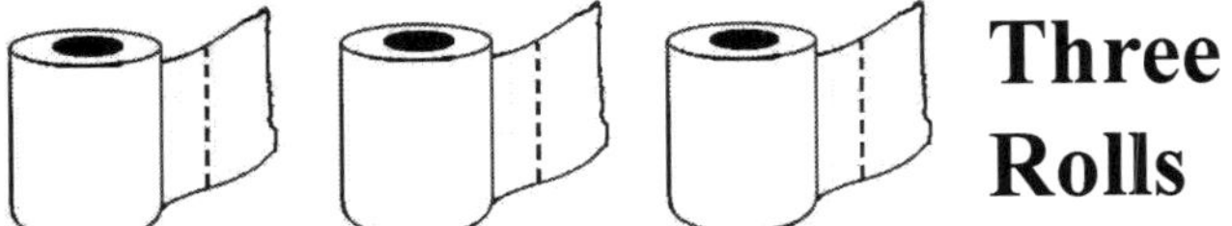

Three Rolls

1. The franchise that became the modern-day Yankees originally played in another city. Ironically, they are now in the same division. Name it.

2. In the 1940s, the Philadelphia Phillies had another unofficial nickname, one currently used by an American League team. What was it?

3. What Negro National League team did Satchel Paige pitch for during most of the 1940s?

4. What league was the National League's competition between 1882-1891? It's initials were AA.

5. Franchise numbers 1 and 2 awarded by the National League in 1876 are still around. Who are they?

6. A "third league" attempted to compete with the NL and AL in 1914 and 1915. What was it called?

7. In the early 1900s, NL teams and AL teams routinely stole each other's players. What current team name resulted from this?

8. According to popular belief, how did the Cleveland Indians get their name around the turn of the 20th century?

9. The first league that is considered "Major League" by the record books lasted from 1871-75. What was it called?

10. Pittsburgh had two powerhouses in the Negro National League. Name one of them.

Answer Sheet

Teams & Leagues
3 Rolls

Name________________

1.
2.
3.
4.
5.
6.
7.
8.
9.
10.

Answer Sheet

Teams & Leagues
3 Rolls

Name________________

1.
2.
3.
4.
5.
6.
7.
8.
9.
10.

Answer Sheet

Teams & Leagues
3 Rolls

Name________________

1.
2.
3.
4.
5.
6.
7.
8.
9.
10.

After you have filled out the sheet, fold your column underneath along the dashed line so the next restroom user won't see your answers. ***The first player uses the far right column.***

Notes:

Notes:

Notes:

Pitchers

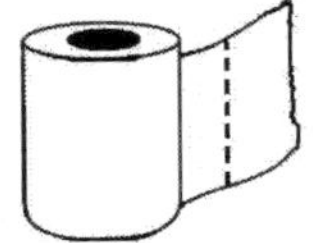

One Roll

Flip to pg. 83 for answers

1. How far is it from the rubber to home plate?

2. What Dodgers pitcher of the 1980s created *Fernandomania*?

3. Who is the only man to win the Cy Young award with four different teams?

4. As of Opening Day, 2012, what team had pitched 35 one-hitters, but zero no-hitters?

5. Whose record of 511 wins will probably never be broken?

6. What Chicago White Sox righthander played on the N.Y. Knickerbockers 1970 and 1973 NBA championship teams?

7. This Texas Rangers reliever was 2010's Rookie-of-the-Year as he recorded 40 saves.

8. Who gave up Bobby Thomson's "Shot Heard 'Round the World" in 1951?

9. What is a screwball?

10. In 2011, Mariano Rivera broke the all-time saves record. Whose record did he break?

Answer Sheet Pitchers 1 Roll	Answer Sheet Pitchers 1 Roll	Answer Sheet Pitchers 1 Roll
Name________	Name________	Name________
1.	1.	1.
2.	2.	2.
3.	3.	3.
4.	4.	4.
5.	5.	5.
6.	6.	6.
7.	7.	7.
8.	8.	8.
9.	9.	9.
10.	10.	10.

After you have filled out the sheet, fold your column underneath along the dashed line so the next restroom user won't see your answers. ***The first player uses the far right column.***

Notes:	***Notes:***	***Notes:***

Pitchers

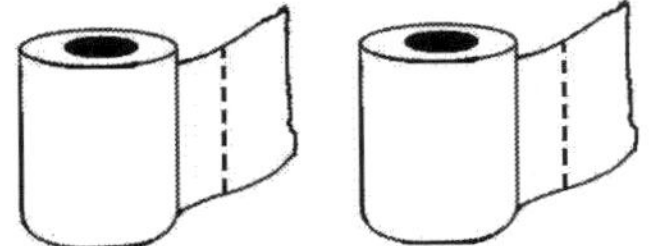

Two Rolls

1. What three categories does pitching's Triple Crown include?

2. Complete this little ditty concerning the Boston Braves' one-two punch in the 1950s. "Spahn and Sain…"

3. Who is the oldest man to ever win a Major League Baseball game?

4. Who is the only pitcher to record a no-hitter on Opening Day?

5. One K separates the AL and NL records for most strikeouts in a season (modern era). Who holds them?

6. This righthander pitched a perfect game for the Phillies against the Mets in 1964, and later became a US Senator from Kentucky.

7. Nolan Ryan has the most career strikeouts with 5,714. Numbers two and three on the all-time list both pitched after 1983. Who are they?

8. Pitching's biggest heartbreak goes to Harvey Haddix on May 26, 1959. What happened?

9. Who was the oldest man to pitch a perfect game?

10. What causes a knuckleball to move so unpredictably?

Answer Sheet Pitchers 2 Rolls	**Answer Sheet** Pitchers 2 Rolls	**Answer Sheet** Pitchers 2 Rolls
Name________________	Name________________	Name________________
1.	1.	1.
2.	2.	2.
3.	3.	3.
4.	4.	4.
5.	5.	5.
6.	6.	6.
7.	7.	7.
8.	8.	8.
9.	9.	9.
10.	10.	10.

After you have filled out the sheet, fold your column underneath along the dashed line so the next restroom user won't see your answers. ***The first player uses the far right column.***

Notes:	***Notes:***	***Notes:***

Pitchers

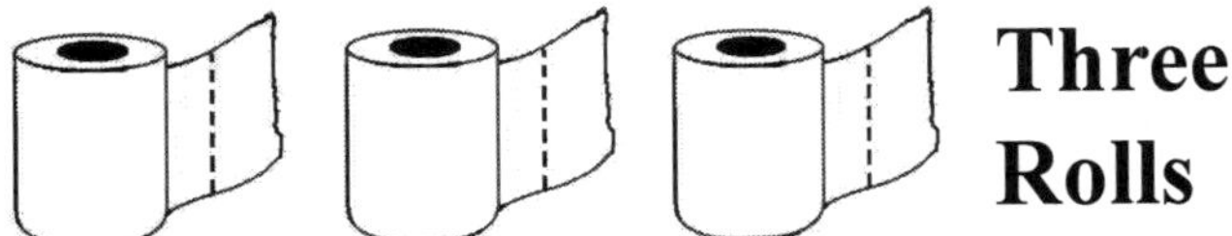

Three Rolls

1. In 1926, this aging Hall of Famer struck out Tony Lazzeri with the bases loaded in the 7th Game of the World Series.

2. In 2011, an American Leaguer and a National Leaguer both won Pitching's Triple Crown. Name them.

3. Who is the only pitcher to hit two grand slam home runs in one game?

4. This crafty lefty has the most complete games in the post-WWII era.

5. When Nolan Ryan first came up to the majors, he used a unique treatment to cure blisters. What was it?

6. Before Justin Verlander in 2011, who was the last pitcher chosen as his league's Most Valuable Player?

7. Two hurlers, who pitched as late as 2009, are in the top 100 for career losses. Who are they?

8. Two Yankees won the Cy Young Award between 1958 and 1961. Who are they?

9. Detroit's Allan Travers gave up 24 runs in his only Major League appearance on May 18,1912. Why was this sandlot player starting a big league game? (The answer involves Ty Cobb.)

10. This big Brooklyn Dodgers righthander won the very first Cy Young Award in 1956 after going 27-7.

Answer Sheet

Pitchers
3 Rolls

Name________________

Answer Sheet

Pitchers
3 Rolls

Name________________

Answer Sheet

Pitchers
3 Rolls

Name________________

1.	1.	1.
2.	2.	2.
3.	3.	3.
4.	4.	4.
5.	5.	5.
6.	6.	6.
7.	7.	7.
8.	8.	8.
9.	9.	9.
10.	10.	10.

After you have filled out the sheet, fold your column underneath along the dashed line so the next restroom user won't see your answers. ***The first player uses the far right column.***

Notes:

Notes:

Notes:

Personalities

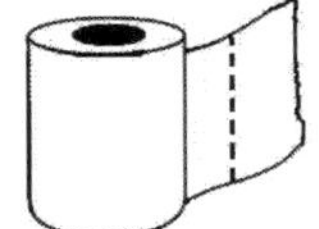

One Roll

1. He's Manny being Manny.

2. Great early Cub first baseman. Tinker to Evers to...

3. Yankee star who reportedly said "déjà vu all over again," and "it gets late early out there."

4. This one-day Major Leaguer was 3 feet, 7 inches tall.

5. He allegedly pointed to center field before his home run in the 1932 World Series.

6. Hall of Fame reliever famous for his handlebar mustache.

7. 1980s-1990s super-athlete who starred for the Kansas City Royals and Oakland Raiders.

8. The Dean brothers of St. Louis.

9. Catcher turned announcer, the worst seats in the ballpark are named for him.

10. He knocked over catcher Ray Fosse to score the winning run in the 1970 All-Star Game.

Answer Sheet Personalities 1 Roll	Answer Sheet Personalities 1 Roll	Answer Sheet Personalities 1 Roll
Name________________	Name________________	Name________________
1.	1.	1.
2.	2.	2.
3.	3.	3.
4.	4.	4.
5.	5.	5.
6.	6.	6.
7.	7.	7.
8.	8.	8.
9.	9.	9.
10.	10.	10.

After you have filled out the sheet, fold your column underneath along the dashed line so the next restroom user won't see your answers. ***The first player uses the far right column.***

Notes:	***Notes:***	***Notes:***

Personalities

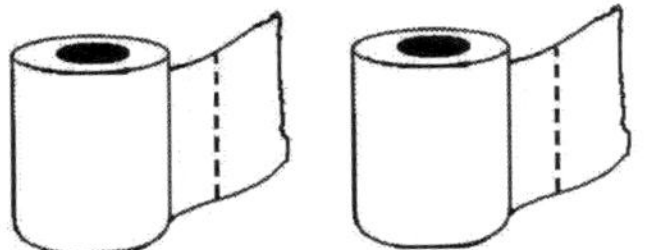

Two Rolls

1. A bird once flew out of his cap on Opening Day. Years later, he was still managing at age 76.

2. What Gold Glove first baseman appeared on the sitcom *Seinfeld*?

3. 1980s-1990s batting champ and Hall of Famer who ate chicken every day.

4. What manager was kicked out of a record 158 games?

5. This Bird enjoyed his injury-shortened career talking to the baseball.

6. A marvelous Met who missed first (and probably second) on his way to a (non) triple.

7. All-around athlete and baseball Hall of Famer, he was drafted by MLB, the NFL, the NBA, and the ABA.

8. Although he holds the third-highest lifetime batting average (.356), this player was banned from baseball for life.

9. This pitcher became a baseball pariah after he wrote his book, *Ball Four*.

10. Name the cigar-chomping baseball executive who invented the farm system, integrated the game, and felt it was better to trade a player too early than too late.

Answer Sheet Personalities 2 Rolls	Answer Sheet Personalities 2 Rolls	Answer Sheet Personalities 2 Rolls
Name__________	Name__________	Name__________
1.	1.	1.
2.	2.	2.
3.	3.	3.
4.	4.	4.
5.	5.	5.
6.	6.	6.
7.	7.	7.
8.	8.	8.
9.	9.	9.
10.	10.	10.

After you have filled out the sheet, fold your column underneath along the dashed line so the next restroom user won't see your answers. ***The first player uses the far right column.***

Notes:	*Notes:*	*Notes:*

Personalities

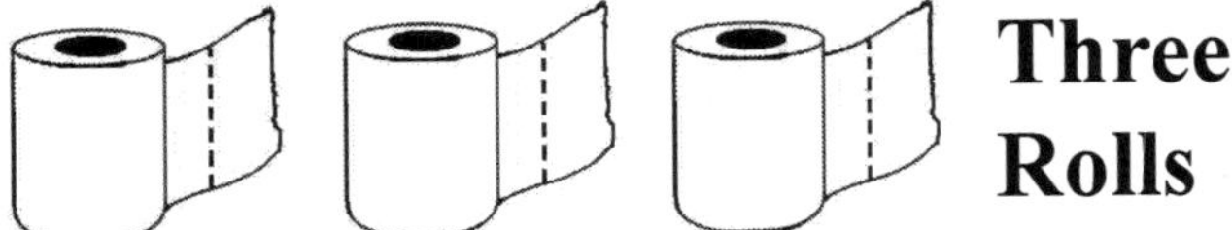

Three Rolls

1. Brooklyn's Babe once put a lit cigar in his baseball pants...and batted .393 in 1930.

2. Fiery shortstop and manager who was famous for giving umpires The Lip.

3. What Mets pitcher set a record by losing 27 straight games in 1992-1993?

4. Name the 1950s-1960s star who ran the bases backwards after his 100th career home run, and was the subject of the movie, *Fear Strikes Out*.

5. Played for the Red Sox and NBA Celtics, he once left the ballclub to try to take a flight to Israel.

6. N.Y. Giants manager who asked facetiously, "Is Brooklyn still in the league?" Unfortunately, he found out by the end of the season that they were.

7. At age 15, he was the youngest player in MLB in the twentieth century.

8. Hall of Fame pitcher who let his catcher, Tim McCarver, do the talking for him.

9. A's owner who promoted white baseball shoes, gold uniforms, and a mule.

10. This former Mets reliever and contemporary pitching coach was known to give teammates "hot foots." Name him.

Answer Sheet Personalities 3 Rolls	Answer Sheet Personalities 3 Rolls	Answer Sheet Personalities 3 Rolls
Name________________	Name________________	Name________________
1.	1.	1.
2.	2.	2.
3.	3.	3.
4.	4.	4.
5.	5.	5.
6.	6.	6.
7.	7.	7.
8.	8.	8.
9.	9.	9.
10.	10.	10.

After you have filled out the sheet, fold your column underneath along the dashed line so the next restroom user won't see your answers. ***The first player uses the far right column.***

Notes:	***Notes:***	***Notes:***

Hall of Fame

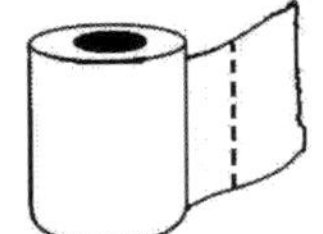

One Roll

1. For how many years must a player be retired to make the Hall of Fame?

2. Who was the first player of Italian ancestry to be elected to the Hall of Fame?

3. There are three Mickeys in the Hall of Fame. Name two of them.

4. Where is the Baseball Hall of Fame located?

5. When it was determined that this slugger would go into the Hall of Fame as an Expo, the Mets gave him a plaque pictured as a Met.

6. There are four players named Robinson in the Hall of Fame. Name three of them.

7. This player was inducted in 1939 shortly after he was diagnosed with a fatal disease that was named after him.

8. This N.Y. Giant great has the shortest last name of anyone in the Hall of Fame.

9. This White Sox executive, whose name adorned the team's ballpark for many years, was inducted in 1939.

10. The L.A. Dodgers of the 1960s had two Hall of Famers in their rotation. Who were they?

Answer Sheet **Hall of Fame** **1 Roll**	**Answer Sheet** **Hall of Fame** **1 Roll**	**Answer Sheet** **Hall of Fame** **1 Roll**
Name________________	**Name**________________	**Name**________________
1.	1.	1.
2.	2.	2.
3.	3.	3.
4.	4.	4.
5.	5.	5.
6.	6.	6.
7.	7.	7.
8.	8.	8.
9.	9.	9.
10.	10.	10.

After you have filled out the sheet, fold your column underneath along the dashed line so the next restroom user won't see your answers. ***The first player uses the far right column.***

Notes:	***Notes:***	***Notes:***

Hall of Fame

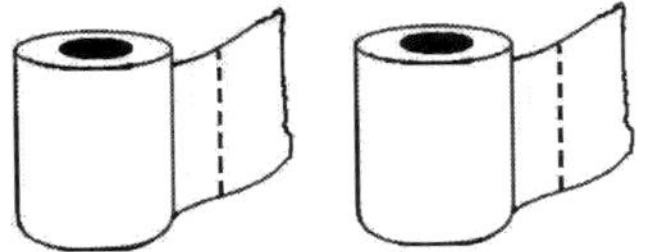

Two Rolls

1. This Cub Hall of Fame duo of the 1950s-1960s never got to taste the World Series.

2. Who was the first Latin American inducted into the Hall of Fame?

3. This Hall of Famer was played in the movies by Ronald Reagan.

4. Who was the first Jewish player inducted into the Hall of Fame?

5. This slugger-turned-broadcaster played only ten years, but was elected to the Hall of Fame in 1975.

6. Two players have gone into the Hall of Fame as Milwaukee Brewers. Who are they?

7. A 1939 inductee is more remembered for his name on sports equipment than for being a pitcher and executive. Who is he?

8. In 1963, this Hall of Famer became the oldest pitcher to win 20+ games in a season.

9. This knuckleballer was the first relief pitcher inducted into the Hall of Fame.

10. This Cub hurler is the only Canadian in the Hall of Fame.

Answer Sheet

Hall of Fame
2 Rolls

Name________________

Answer Sheet

Hall of Fame
2 Rolls

Name________________

Answer Sheet

Hall of Fame
2 Rolls

Name________________

1.	1.	1.
2.	2.	2.
3.	3.	3.
4.	4.	4.
5.	5.	5.
6.	6.	6.
7.	7.	7.
8.	8.	8.
9.	9.	9.
10.	10.	10.

After you have filled out the sheet, fold your column underneath along the dashed line so the next restroom user won't see your answers. ***The first player uses the far right column.***

Notes:

Notes:

Notes:

Hall of Fame

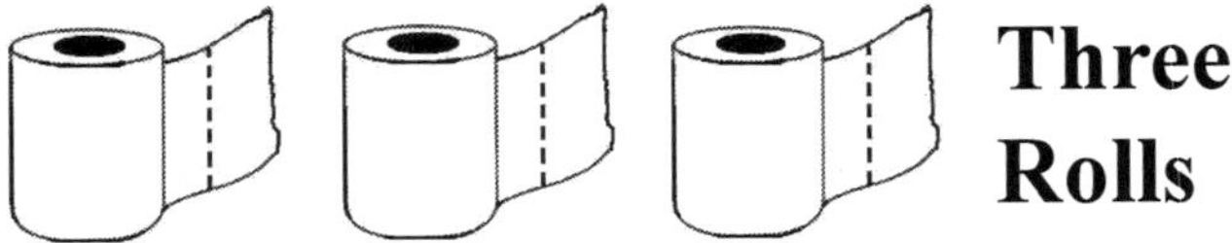

Three Rolls

1. There is only one Hall of Famer whose last name begins with "I." Who is he?

2. In 1937, the first two managers were inducted. Who were they?

3. Within three, how many umpires have been inducted into the Hall of Fame?

4. The first five inductees were elected to the Hall of Fame in 1936. Name four of them.

5. What Hall of Famer took a check for a million dollars and hung it on his wall instead of cashing it?

6. This late-20th century Hall of Fame manager won World Series titles with a team in each league.

7. This dazzling pitcher was the first Brooklyn Dodger inducted into the Hall of Fame.

8. This turn of the 20th century Hall of Famer "Hit 'em where they ain't."

9. This mean-spirited player-manager of the 19th century Chicago White Stockings helped create baseball's notorious color line. Nonetheless, he was inducted in 1939.

10. Both members of the White Sox double play combo of the 1950s-1960s are in the Hall of Fame. Name one of them.

Answer Sheet Hall of Fame 3 Rolls Name________________	**Answer Sheet** Hall of Fame 3 Rolls Name________________	**Answer Sheet** Hall of Fame 3 Rolls Name________________
1.	1.	1.
2.	2.	2.
3.	3.	3.
4.	4.	4.
5.	5.	5.
6.	6.	6.
7.	7.	7.
8.	8.	8.
9.	9.	9.
10.	10.	10.

After you have filled out the sheet, fold your column underneath along the dashed line so the next restroom user won't see your answers. ***The first player uses the far right column.***

Notes:	***Notes:***	***Notes:***

World Series

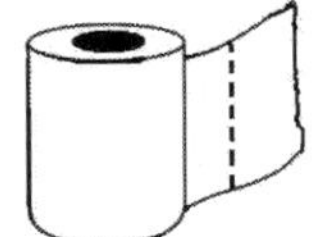

One Roll

1. What player appeared in the most World Series games?

2. Who hit the ball that went through Bill Buckner's legs in 1986?

3. When was the last time the Chicago Cubs won the World Series?

4. The Yankees have won the most World Series (27). Who has won the second most?

5. Which manager has won the most World Series games?

6. Who was the manager of the 1969 "Miracle Mets?"

7. Who stole home in Game 1 of the 1955 World Series for the Brooklyn Dodgers?

8. Who has the most lifetime World Series home runs?

9. Why was there no World Series in 1994?

10. In 2009, this Phillies slugger set a record by striking out 13 times in the World Series.

Answer Sheet World Series 1 Roll	Answer Sheet World Series 1 Roll	Answer Sheet World Series 1 Roll
Name________________	Name________________	Name________________
1.	1.	1.
2.	2.	2.
3.	3.	3.
4.	4.	4.
5.	5.	5.
6.	6.	6.
7.	7.	7.
8.	8.	8.
9.	9.	9.
10.	10.	10.

After you have filled out the sheet, fold your column underneath along the dashed line so the next restroom user won't see your answers. ***The first player uses the far right column.***

Notes:	***Notes:***	***Notes:***

World Series

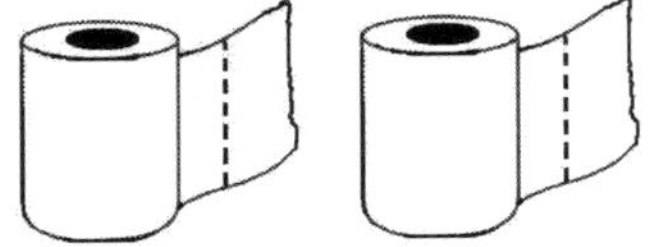

Two Rolls

1. Who were the opponents in the first World Series in 1903?

2. The 1921 and 1922 World Series was played in one ballpark. Who were the opponents for both Series?

3. Who hit the ball that Willie Mays made the great over-the-shoulder catch in the 1954 World Series?

4. Which team, founded in 1883, waited until 1980 to win its first World Series?

5. This player stole a record 7 bases in a World Series twice.

6. In 2001, this lefty won three games in the World Series. It marked the last time this feat has been done.

7. A Red Sox infielder, a Yankee infielder, and a Cardinal outfielder hold the record of 13 hits in a Series. Name two of them.

8. Who beat the Chicago White Sox in the 1919 World Series when the Sox were bought out by gamblers?

9. In 1903, 1919, 1920, and 1921, how many games did a team have to win to clinch the Series?

10. What was unique about Game 4 of the 1971 World Series between Baltimore and Pittsburgh?

Answer Sheet World Series 2 Rolls	Answer Sheet World Series 2 Rolls	Answer Sheet World Series 2 Rolls
Name________________	Name________________	Name________________
1.	1.	1.
2.	2.	2.
3.	3.	3.
4.	4.	4.
5.	5.	5.
6.	6.	6.
7.	7.	7.
8.	8.	8.
9.	9.	9.
10.	10.	10.

After you have filled out the sheet, fold your column underneath along the dashed line so the next restroom user won't see your answers. ***The first player uses the far right column.***

Notes:	***Notes:***	***Notes:***

World Series

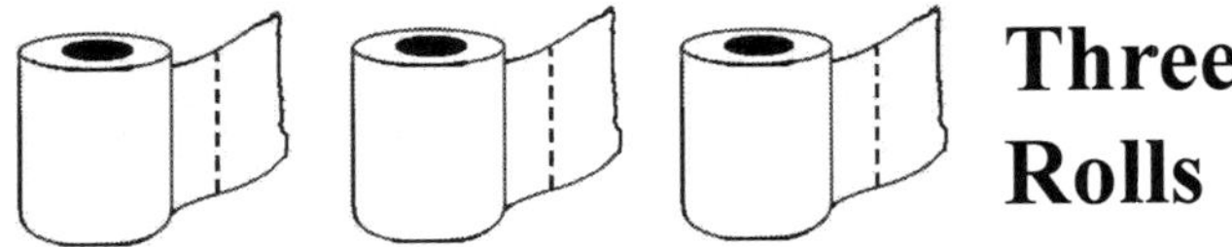

Three Rolls

1. Why was there no World Series in 1904?

2. The 1944 World Series was played in one ballpark. Who were the opponents?

3. What team hosted the first World Series game to be held indoors?

4. Within two years either way, when was the World Series first televised nationally?

5. Who was the last Dodger manager to win the World Series?

6. Who is the only player to pull off an unassisted triple play in the World Series?

7. How are Dodger Cookie Lavagetto and Yankee Floyd (Bill) Bevens linked together in World Series folklore?

8. This 1970s Cincinnati Reds relief pitcher has the lowest career ERA in World Series history (Min. 20 innings).

9. Although he had a lifetime batting average of .264, this Cincinnati Red named Billy has the highest batting average in a World Series (.750).

10. This Yankees infielder holds the record for most RBI in a World Series.

Answer Sheet **World Series** **3 Rolls**	**Answer Sheet** **World Series** **3 Rolls**	**Answer Sheet** **World Series** **3 Rolls**
Name________________	**Name**________________	**Name**________________
1.	1.	1.
2.	2.	2.
3.	3.	3.
4.	4.	4.
5.	5.	5.
6.	6.	6.
7.	7.	7.
8.	8.	8.
9.	9.	9.
10.	10.	10.

After you have filled out the sheet, fold your column underneath along the dashed line so the next restroom user won't see your answers. ***The first player uses the far right column.***

Notes:	***Notes:***	***Notes:***

Everything & Anything

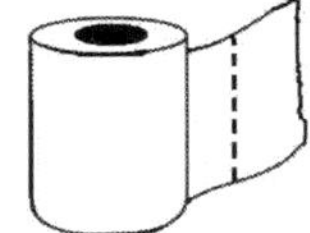

One Roll

1. What famous oil company sign looms beyond Boston's Green Monster?

2. Before Sept. 1st, how many players may be on a Major League team's active roster?

3. In what state was Kevin Costner's *Field of Dreams* located?

4. What does a backwards "K" mean on a scorecard?

5. Who was the Yankee Stadium PA announcer for 56 years?

6. What is a "can of corn?"

7. This broadcaster was famous for his 7th inning rendition of *Take Me Out to the Ballgame.*

8. What non-baseball equipment did catcher Charlie O'Brien use to protect his face?

9. Who played Willie Mays Hayes in the movie, *Major League*?

10. When Carl Yastrzemski led the AL in batting with a .301 average in 1968, what did baseball do to increase offense?

Answer Sheet	Answer Sheet	Answer Sheet
Everything & Anything 1 Roll	Everything & Anything 1 Roll	Everything & Anything 1 Roll
Name________________	Name________________	Name________________
1.	1.	1.
2.	2.	2.
3.	3.	3.
4.	4.	4.
5.	5.	5.
6.	6.	6.
7.	7.	7.
8.	8.	8.
9.	9.	9.
10.	10.	10.

After you have filled out the sheet, fold your column underneath along the dashed line so the next restroom user won't see your answers. ***The first player uses the far right column.***

Notes:	***Notes:***	***Notes:***

Everything & Anything

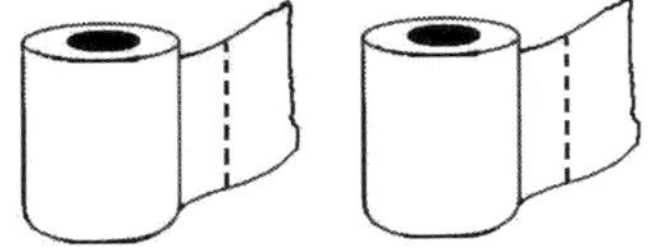

Two Rolls

Flip to pg. 96 for answers

1. You make the call. A ground ball dribbles into foul territory and then comes back into fair territory before reaching third base. Is it fair or foul?

2. Whose lawsuit against Major League Baseball opened the door to free agency?

3. Who was the unanimous choice for AL Rookie-of-the-Year in 1987 after batting .289 with 49 home runs and 118 RBI?

4. Why was the N.Y. Giants' incredible comeback in late 1951 probably tainted?

5. Before the first modern expansion in the early 1960s, how many games made up the regular season?

6. Two men have hit 5 home runs in a doubleheader. Name one of them.

7. Who was the one-armed outfielder who played for the St. Louis Browns in 1945?

8. What was the last MLB team to place an African American player on its roster?

9. What team owner was famous for a midget and exploding scoreboards?

10. Who was the first designated hitter?

Answer Sheet	Answer Sheet	Answer Sheet
Everything & Anything **2 Rolls**	**Everything & Anything** **2 Rolls**	**Everything & Anything** **2 Rolls**
Name________________	**Name**________________	**Name**________________
1.	1.	1.
2.	2.	2.
3.	3.	3.
4.	4.	4.
5.	5.	5.
6.	6.	6.
7.	7.	7.
8.	8.	8.
9.	9.	9.
10.	10.	10.

After you have filled out the sheet, fold your column underneath along the dashed line so the next restroom user won't see your answers. ***The first player uses the far right column.***

Notes:	***Notes:***	***Notes:***

Everything & Anything

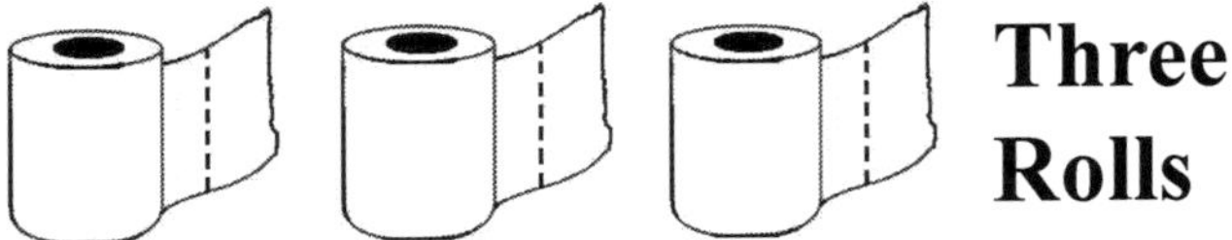

Three Rolls

1. What did Dodgers announcer Red Barber mean in the 1940s when he said that the bases were FOB?

2. This famous 19th century concessionaire is sometimes given credit for putting hot dogs inside of buns.

3. You make the call. A fly ball hits off a fielder's glove in fair territory and lands in the stands in foul territory. What is it?

4. The rarest of baseball events, there have been only 15 of these in modern baseball history.

5. There are several ways a batter can reach first base safely. Name six of them.

6. In the 1949 movie, *It Happens Every Spring*, what did Ray Milland's character accidentally discover which enabled him to become a great pitcher?

7. How wide is home plate?

8. Within ten, how many (double) stitches are there on a baseball?

9. What was the only MLB season to be shortened by war?

10. How can one person be both the winning pitcher and losing pitcher in the same game?

Answer Sheet Everything & Anything 3 Rolls	Answer Sheet Everything & Anything 3 Rolls	Answer Sheet Everything & Anything 3 Rolls
Name________________	Name________________	Name________________
1.	1.	1.
2.	2.	2.
3.	3.	3.
4.	4.	4.
5.	5.	5.
6.	6.	6.
7.	7.	7.
8.	8.	8.
9.	9.	9.
10.	10.	10.

After you have filled out the sheet, fold your column underneath along the dashed line so the next restroom user won't see your answers. ***The first player uses the far right column.***

Notes:	***Notes:***	***Notes:***

Great Moments

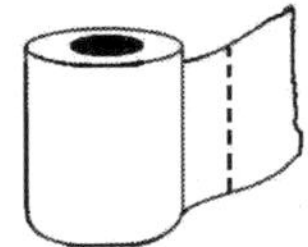

One Roll — Answers

1. Hank Aaron passed Babe Ruth with his 715th career home run

2. Roy Halladay vs. the Cincinnati Reds

3. He struck out 20 batters. He did it first on April 29, 1986 vs. the Seattle Mariners. This time he did it against the Detroit Tigers.

4. He pitched his seventh—and final—no hitter

5. Tom Seaver

6. He set a World Series record with 17 strikeouts

7. Don Larsen

8. Mickey Mantle

9. Joe Carter

10. Roger Maris, who hit his 61st home run of the season, eclipsing Babe Ruth's long-standing record

Great Moments

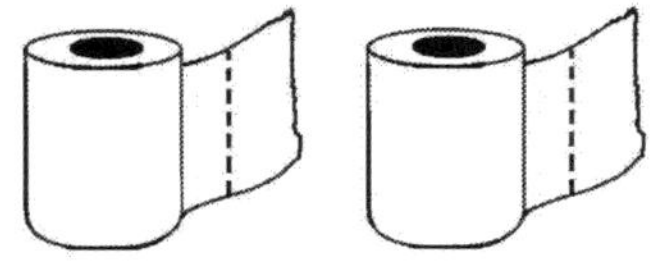

Two Rolls — Answers

1. Injured Dodger Kirk Gibson came off the bench to hit a game-winning, pinch hit home run against the Oakland A's in Game 1 of the World Series

2. Denny McLain

3. Bill Mazeroski

4. On Aug. 8, 1988, the game against Philadelphia was called by rain after 3½ innings. The next night the Cubs beat the Mets 6-4.

5. Minnesota Twins

6. David Ortiz

7. He hit a home run in his final at bat into the bullpen at Fenway Park

8. Johnny Vander Meer of Cincinnati pitched his second consecutive no-hitter

9. Carl Hubbell. After two men reached base, he utilized his screwball to strike out, in order, Babe Ruth, Lou Gehrig, Jimmie Foxx, Al Simmons, and Joe Cronin.

10. His 56-game hitting streak came to an end

Great Moments

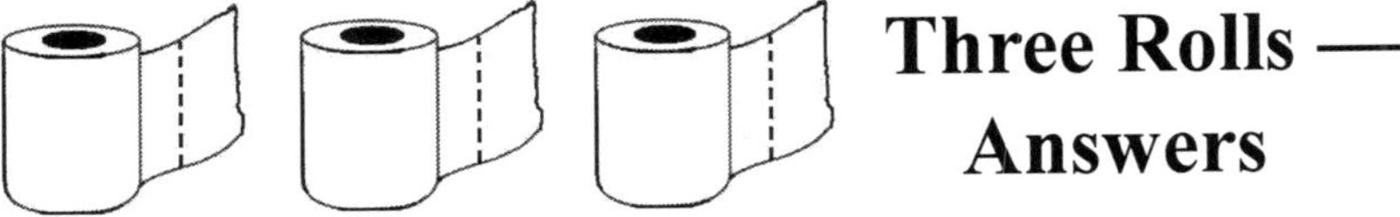

Three Rolls — Answers

1. Fred Lynn in 1983

2. The game lasted 26 innings and ended in a 1-1 tie. The length of the game was 3:50. Today, Yankees-Red Sox 9-inning games take longer! It was the longest game by innings in Major League history.

3. Tommie Agee

4. Pat Darcy

5. Nobody out. Hank DeBerry at third, Dazzy Vance at second, Chick Fewster at first. Babe Herman hits a long gapper to right. DeBerry scores. Vance rounds third, stops, and slides back. Fewster also rounds third and goes back. Herman is not watching and he too, slides into third. The correct ruling is that Vance is safe; Fewster and Herman are out. Originally it was thought that Herman "tripled into a triple play," but he only "doubled into a double play."

6. Eric Show

7. Enos Slaughter

8. Fred Merkle was on first. A single brought in the apparent winning run from third. However Merkle did not touch second base and went straight to the clubhouse in centerfield. He was ultimately called out. The game was ruled a tie, and was replayed on Oct. 8th with the Cubs and Giants tied for first. Chicago won that game...and the pennant.

9. Gabby Hartnett's home run vs. Pittsburgh on Sept. 28, 1938 in the dusk of unlit Wrigley Field helped the Cubs later win the pennant

10. They each pitched 9 innings of no-hit ball. Vaughn gave up a couple of hits and a run in the 10th as the Reds won the game.

Ballparks

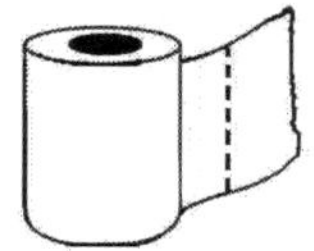

One Roll — Answers

1. Los Angeles Memorial Coliseum

2. Forbes Field

3. Oriole Park at Camden Yards

4. The Astrodome

5. The Green Monster

6. Wrigley Field

7. Veterans Stadium, or "The Vet"

8. San Francisco, at AT&T Park

9. Yankee Stadium

10. Chase Field. If you said its previous name, Bank One Ballpark, you are correct.

Ballparks

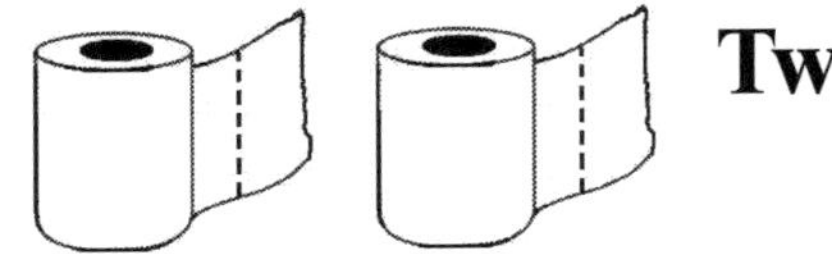

Two Rolls — Answers

1. It marks one mile above sea level

2. Polo Grounds

3. Houston's Enron Field. It's now called Minute Maid Park.

4. Briggs Stadium

5. Comiskey Park on Disco Demolition Night—July 12, 1979

6. San Diego's Jack Murphy Stadium

7. Dodger Stadium

8. Ebbets Field

9. Shea Stadium

10. Toronto's Sky Dome, now called Rogers Centre. The very first retractable dome was at Olympic Stadium in Montreal. It hardly ever worked.

Ballparks

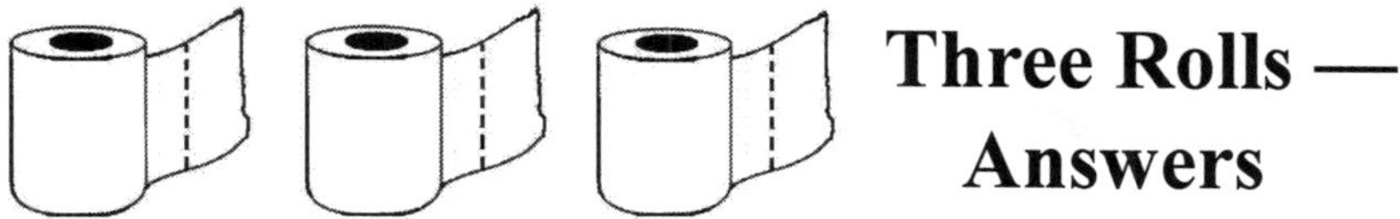

Three Rolls — Answers

1. Polo Grounds. They shared it with the Giants.

2. Griffith Stadium in Washington, DC

3. The Federal League Chicago Whales in 1914. It was called Weeghman Park.

4. Jacobs Field replaced Cleveland Municipal Stadium

5. Bernie Brewer. At old Milwaukee County Stadium, he slid into a gigantic mug of beer. Today he is alcohol-free.

6. The Allegheny, the Monongahela, and the Ohio

7. "Greenberg Gardens" for Hank Greenberg; "Kiner's Korner" for Ralph Kiner

8. Crosley Field

9. Jarry Park (or Parc Jarry)

10. Sportsman's Park. It was home to both the Cardinals and the Browns.

Hitters

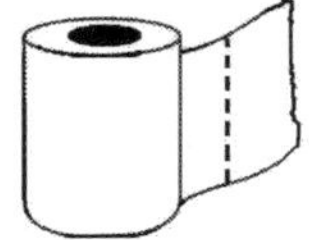

One Roll — Answers

1. Batting fourth in the lineup
2. Rickey Henderson—81
3. The Yankees of the 1920s
4. He gets a single, double, triple, and home run in the same game
5. Roberto Clemente
6. Reggie Jackson—2,597 K's. The only one on the radar is Jim Thome with 2,487 K's going into the 2012 season.
7. Barry Bonds
8. The batter's maximum power zone
9. Lou Gehrig
10. He's up after the on-deck hitter

Hitters

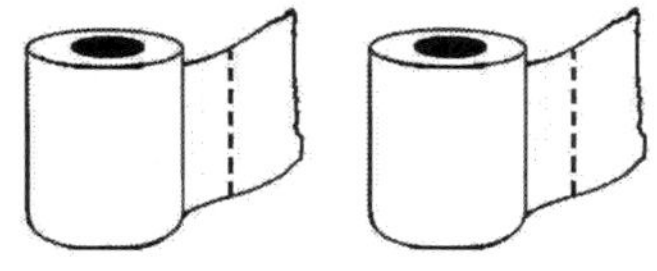

Two Rolls — Answers

1. Ty Cobb (.366), Rogers Hornsby (.358), Joe Jackson (.356)
2. Lou Brock
3. 4 feet by 6 feet. Same dimensions as a hockey net.
4. Strike. And the ball is dead.
5. Yogi Berra and Roy Campanella
6. Striking out 4 (or more) times in a game
7. Jimmie Foxx (1932) and Hank Greenberg (1938)
8. 2,130
9. Carl Yastrzemski in 1967
10. Ash

Hitters

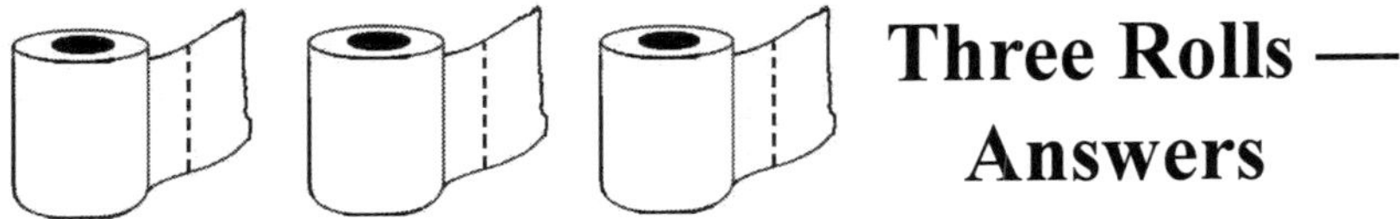

Three Rolls — Answers

1. Grounding into double plays. He did it 350 times.

2. Babe Ruth, Willie Mays, Sammy Sosa, Jimmie Foxx, Mel Ott

3. Tony Gwynn - .338

4. Craig Biggio

5. Jose Canseco, Alex Rodriguez, Barry Bonds, Alfonso Soriano

6. George Brett—.390 in 1980. Tony Gwynn batted .394 in the strike-shortened season of 1994, which really doesn't count for the record books. However if you said either, give yourself the points.

7. Javy Lopez. He hit one additional home run as a pinch hitter.

8. That was the only year when walks counted as hits

9. He went 7 for 7

10. Rogers Hornsby and Ted Williams

Nicknames

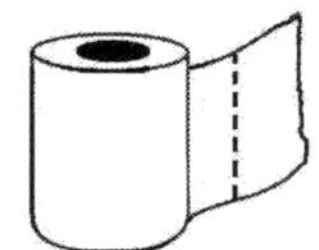

One Roll — Answers

1.George Herman "Babe" Ruth

2. Pete Rose

3. Joe DiMaggio

4. Alex Rodriguez

5. Leroy "Satchel" Paige

6. Hank Aaron

7. Félix Hernandez

8. Harold "Pee Wee" Reese

9. David Ortiz

10. Ty Cobb

Nicknames

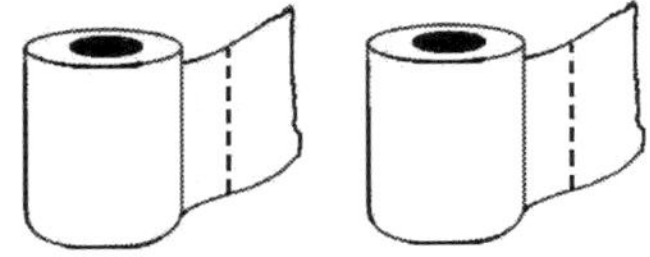

Two Rolls — Answers

1. Harmon Killebrew
2. Carlton Fisk or Ivan Rodriguez
3. Ozzie Smith
4. Casey Stengel
5. Duke Snider
6. Phil Rizzuto
7. Francisco Rodriguez
8. Dwight Gooden
9. Ted Williams
10. Ernie Banks

Nicknames

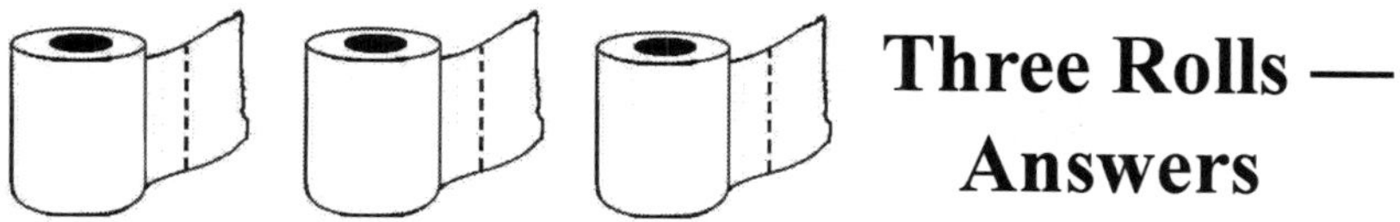

Three Rolls — Answers

1. Joe Medwick

2. Enos Slaughter

3. Juan Marichal

4. Walter Johnson

5. Christy Mathewson. “Big Six” was the name of a famous New York City fire truck used by the political machine, Tammany Hall.

6. James “Cool Papa” Bell

7. Frankie Frisch

8. Johnny “Pepper” Martin

9. Harold “Pie” Traynor

10. Bob Feller

Teams & Leagues

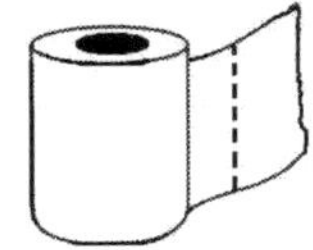

One Roll — Answers

1. St. Louis Cardinals
2. Philadelphia Athletics
3. The Chicago White Sox, who fixed the 1919 World Series
4. Colt .45s
5. The Dodgers
6. Montreal Expos
7. The original Washington Senators
8. New York Knights
9. Colorado Rockies
10. Milwaukee Brewers

Teams & Leagues

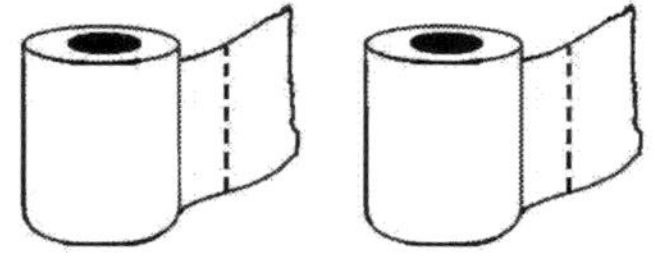

Two Rolls — Answers

1. Chicago White Sox

2. Arizona Diamondbacks in 2001

3. St. Louis Wolves

4. Seattle Pilots

5. St. Louis Browns

6. Chicago. The 1871 Chicago White Stockings had to spend the last part of the season on the road as a result of the Great Chicago Fire.

7. New York Metropolitans, or Mets

8. Highlanders

9. Brooklyn Dodgers

10. Boston Braves

Teams & Leagues

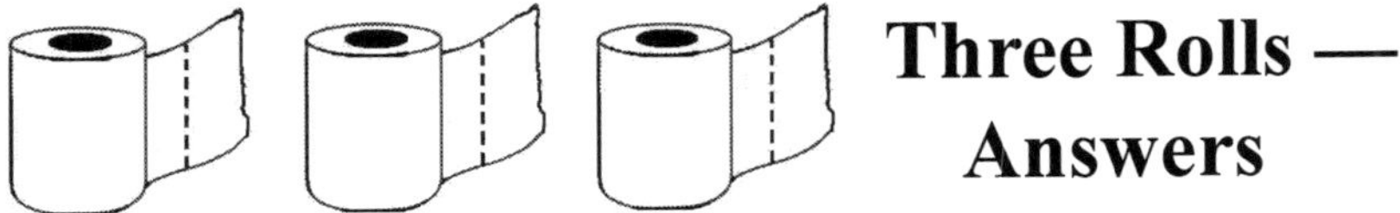

Three Rolls — Answers

1. Baltimore. They were the original Baltimore Orioles.

2. Blue Jays

3. Kansas City Monarchs

4. American Association

5. Boston Red Stockings (now the Atlanta Braves) and Chicago White Stockings (now the Cubs)

6. The Federal League

7. Pittsburgh Pirates

8. Many historians feel that the old Cleveland Spiders of the NL were also called the Indians because of their Native American player, Louis Sockalexis. The name carried over to the AL team.

9. The National Association

10. The Crawfords and the Homestead Grays

Pitchers

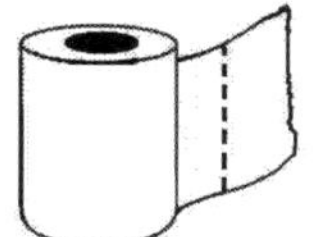

One Roll — Answers

1. 60 feet 6 inches

2. Fernando Valenzuela

3. Roger Clemens—Red Sox, Blue Jays, Yankees, and Astros

4. N.Y. Mets. But finally on June 1, 2012, Johan Santana ended the drought by pitching a no-no against the St. Louis Cardinals.

5. Cy Young

6. Dave DeBusschere

7. Neftali Feliz

8. Ralph Branca

9. A ball that breaks in the opposite direction. For a righthander, it will break to the right, the opposite of a curve ball.

10. Trevor Hoffman

Pitchers

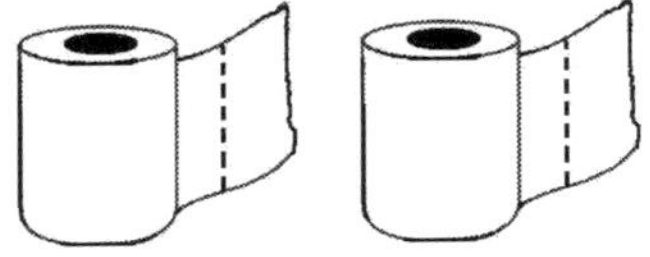

Two Rolls — Answers

1. Wins, Strikeouts, Earned Run Average

2. "...and pray for rain."

3. On April 17, 2012, Jamie Moyer broke Brooklyn Dodger Jack Quinn's record when he won a game for the Rockies at age 49 years, 150 days. Quinn was 49 years, 74 days old.

4. Bob Feller for Cleveland in 1940 against the Chicago White Sox

5. Nolan Ryan (383 in the AL), Sandy Koufax (382 in the NL)

6. Jim Bunning

7. Randy Johnson—4,875 K's, Roger Clemens—4,672 K's

8. He pitched 12 perfect innings, only to lose the game in the 13th

9. Randy Johnson on May 18, 2004 at age 40

10. The ball has no spin, causing wind currents to act on it randomly

Pitchers

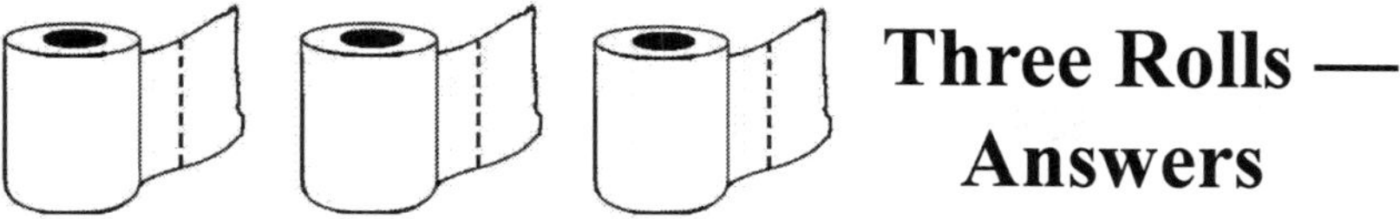

Three Rolls — Answers

1. Grover Cleveland Alexander

2. Justin Verlander of the Tigers and Clayton Kershaw of the Dodgers

3. Tony Cloninger of the Milwaukee Braves on July 3, 1966

4. Warren Spahn with 382

5. He would soak his fingers in pickle brine

6. Oakland's Dennis Eckersley in 1992

7. Entering the 2012 season, Jamie Moyer had 204 losses. Randy Johnson finished his career with 166 losses.

8. Bob Turley (1958) and Whitey Ford (1961)

9. Ty Cobb was suspended for attacking a fan. His teammates went on strike (surprisingly) to support him. Rather than forfeit, the Tigers management found a bunch of college and sandlot players to fill in for one game. Travers later became a priest.

10. Don Newcombe

Personalities

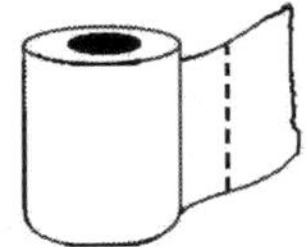

One Roll — Answers

1. Manny Ramírez
2. Frank Chance
3. Yogi Berra
4. Eddie Gaedel
5. Babe Ruth
6. Rollie Fingers
7. Bo Jackson
8. Dizzy and Daffy (Jay and Paul)
9. Bob Uecker
10. Pete Rose

Personalities

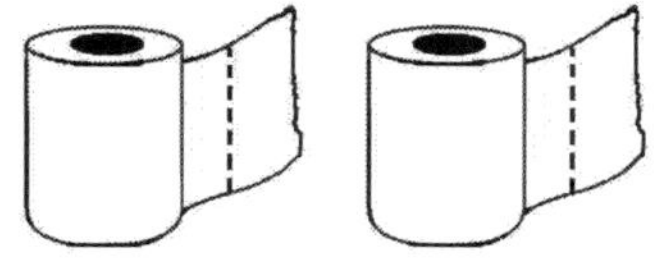

Two Rolls — Answers

1. Casey Stengel

2. Keith Hernandez

3. Wade Boggs

4. Bobby Cox. And he was kicked out of three post-season games as well.

5. Mark "The Bird" Fidrych

6. Marvelous Marv Throneberry

7. Dave Winfield

8. Shoeless Joe Jackson, who by the way, only went "shoeless" once—in an exhibition game. His new cleats didn't fit well. The name stuck.

9. Jim Bouton

10. Branch Rickey

Personalities

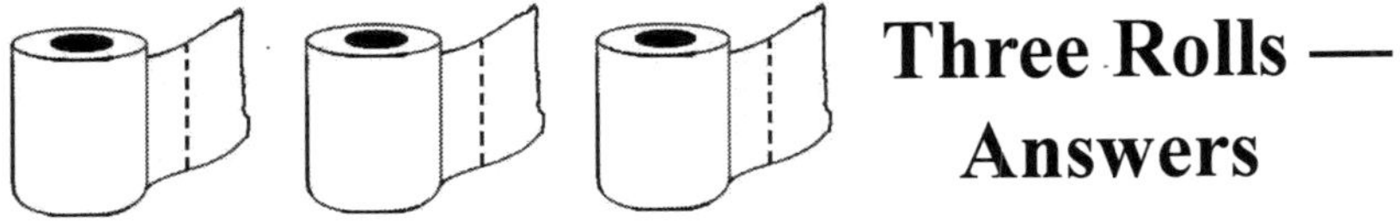

Three Rolls — Answers

1. Floyd "Babe" Herman

2. Leo "The Lip" Durocher

3. Anthony Young

4. Jimmy Piersall

5. Gene Conley

6. Bill Terry. Before the 1934 season, a writer asked the Giants' manager about the Dodgers' chances in the pennant race. He answered, "Is Brooklyn still in the league?" On the last weekend of the season, the sixth place Dodgers took two straight at the Polo Grounds to knock their rivals out of the pennant race.

7. Joe Nuxhall

8. Steve Carlton

9. Charlie Finley

10. Roger McDowell. He would set players' shoes on fire when they weren't looking.

Hall of Fame

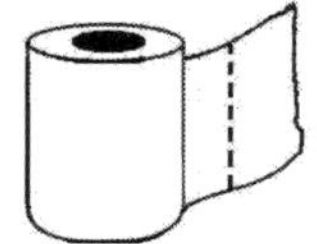

One Roll — Answers

1. Five years

2. Joe DiMaggio in 1955

3. Mickey Cochrane, Mickey Mantle, and Mickey Welch. If you never heard of Mickey Welch, he was a pitcher in the 1880s and 1890s.

4. Cooperstown, NY

5. Gary Carter

6. Brooks Robinson, Frank Robinson, Jackie Robinson, Wilbert Robinson

7. Lou Gehrig. Interestingly enough, some doctors have recently hypothesized that he did not have ALS, or "Lou Gehrig's Disease," but rather an equally fatal malady caused by numerous concussions.

8. Mel Ott

9. Charles Comiskey

10. Sandy Koufax and Don Drysdale

Hall of Fame

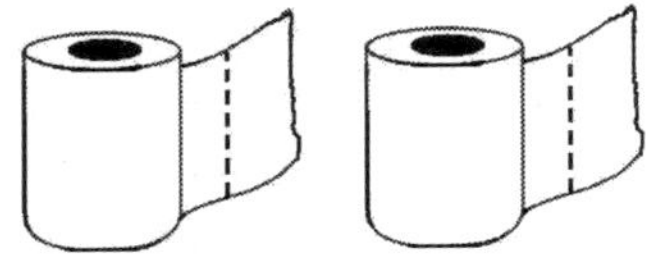

Two Rolls — Answers

1. Ernie Banks and Billy Williams
2. Roberto Clemente in 1973
3. Grover Cleveland Alexander
4. Hank Greenberg in 1956
5. Ralph Kiner
6. Robin Yount and Paul Molitor
7. Albert Goodwill Spalding
8. Warren Spahn
9. Hoyt Wilhelm
10. Ferguson Jenkins

Hall of Fame

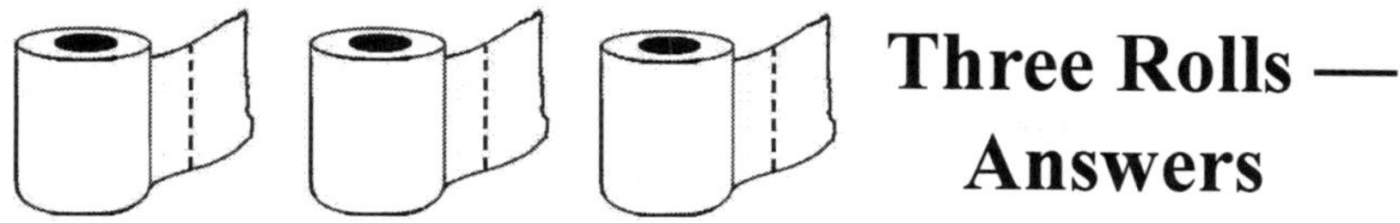

Three Rolls — Answers

1. Monte Irvin

2. Connie Mack and John McGraw

3. Nine

4. Ty Cobb, Walter Johnson, Christy Mathewson, Babe Ruth, and Honus Wagner

5. Rickey Henderson. He finally got around to cashing it a few months later, but he wanted to remind himself that he was a millionaire. The A's asked him to cash it for record-keeping purposes.

6. Sparky Anderson. He won with the Cincinnati Reds in 1975 and 1976, and with the Detroit Tigers in 1984.

7. Dazzy Vance

8. Wee Willie Keeler

9. Cap Anson

10. Luis Aparicio and Nellie Fox

World Series

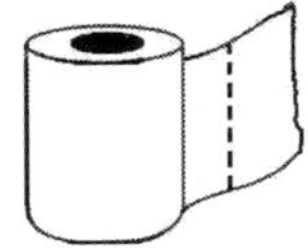

One Roll — Answers

1. Yogi Berra—75
2. Mookie Wilson
3. 1908
4. St. Louis Cardinals—10
5. Casey Stengel—37. Which just happens to be his uniform number.
6. Gil Hodges
7. Jackie Robinson
8. Mickey Mantle—18
9. There was a players' strike
10. Ryan Howard

World Series

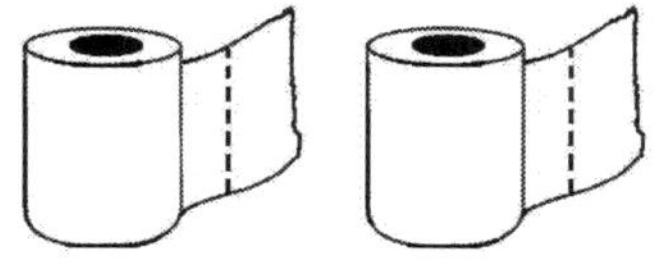

Two Rolls — Answers

1. Boston Americans vs. Pittsburgh Pirates. If you said anything with Boston and Pittsburgh, that's fine.

2. All games between the N.Y. Giants and N.Y. Yankees were played at the Polo Grounds, home field for both

3. Vic Wertz

4. Philadelphia Phillies

5. Lou Brock in the 1967 and 1968 World Series

6. Randy Johnson

7. Marty Barrett, Bobby Richardson, Lou Brock

8. Cincinnati Reds

9. Five

10. It was the first World Series game played at night

World Series

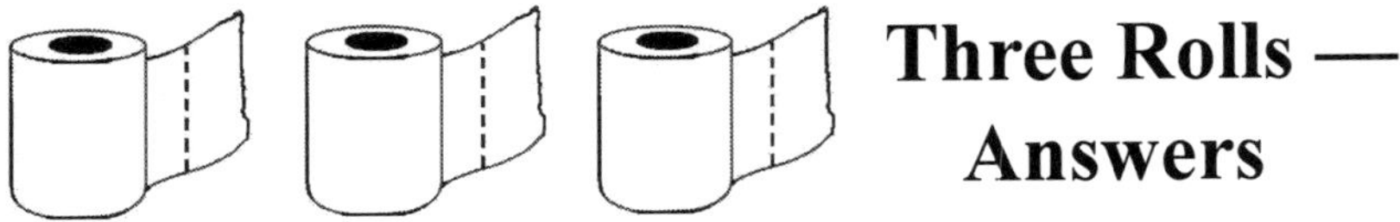

Three Rolls — Answers

1. John McGraw's N.Y. Giants refused to play the Boston Americans

2. All games between the St. Louis Cardinals and St. Louis Browns were played at Sportsman's Park, home field for both

3. The Minnesota Twins, who opposed the St. Louis Cardinals in 1987

4. The 1947 World Series between the N.Y. Yankees and Brooklyn Dodgers

5. Tom Lasorda in 1988

6. Bill Wambsganss for Cleveland in the 1920 World Series against Brooklyn. Pitcher Clarence Mitchell hit the ball.

7. Lavagetto's walk off double broke up Bevens' no-hit bid with two out in the 9th inning of Game Four of the 1947 World Series. Brooklyn won the game 3-2, but the Yankees won the Series.

8. Jack Billingham

9. Billy Hatcher in 1990 vs. Oakland. He also set a World Series record with 7 straight hits.

10. Bobby Richardson—12 in 1960

Everything & Anything

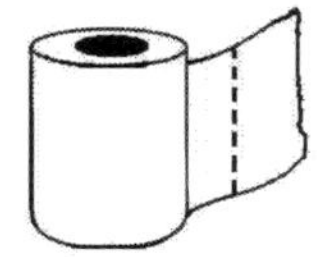

One Roll — Answers

1. Citgo
2. 25
3. Iowa
4. Strike three looking
5. Bob Sheppard
6. A lazy fly ball
7. Harry Caray
8. Hockey goalie's mask
9. Wesley Snipes
10. The pitcher's mound was lowered from 15" to 10"

Everything & Anything

Two Rolls — Answers

1. Fair ball

2. Cardinals outfielder Curt Flood

3. Mark McGwire

4. They allegedly stole signs. From about mid-season on, Giants personnel viewed catchers' signs from the centerfield clubhouse at the Polo Grounds. They were relayed to the bullpen, which was located in the deep outfield, via an electric buzzer. The bullpen catcher would then cross or uncross his legs to indicate a fastball or a curveball.

5. 154 games

6. Stan Musial and Nate Colbert

7. Pete Gray. He batted .218 in 77 games.

8. Boston Red Sox. Pumpsie Green joined the team in 1959.

9. Bill Veeck

10. Ron Blomberg of the N.Y. Yankees on April 6, 1973

Everything & Anything

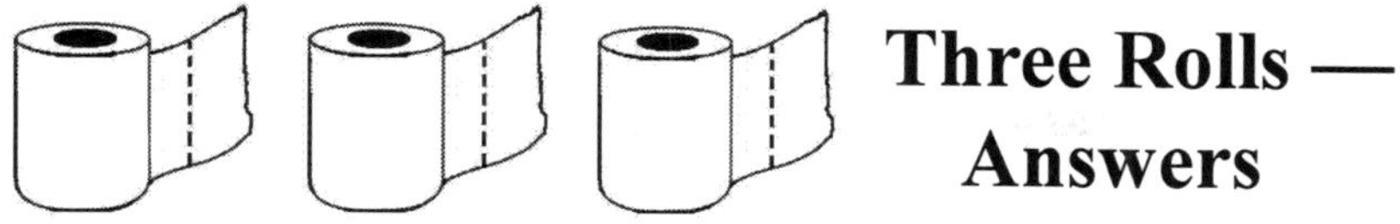

Three Rolls — Answers

1. Full of Brooklyns

2. Harry M. Stevens

3. A double

4. Unassisted Triple Play

5. Hit, walk, intentional walk, hit by pitch, error, dropped third strike, catcher interference, fielder interference, fielder's choice (force out), spectator interference, hitting a runner with a batted ball. There are other obscure ways, but these are the most common.

6. A compound which made a baseball repel wood, making it impossible to hit

7. 17 inches

8. 108 double stiches

9. 1918, during World War I. Teams played about 126 games.

10. Hypothetical situation: Los Angeles is at Chicago on May 15th. Smith is pitching for Chicago and has pitched the entire game, which is scoreless through eight innings. Los Angeles scores a run off of Smith in the top of the ninth. After three outs, it starts to rain, and the game is eventually stopped. Because Chicago hasn't batted in the bottom of the ninth, it is a suspended game. The teams will play next on August 18th, at which time the game will be resumed where it left off. In the interim, Smith is traded from Chicago to Los Angeles. When the game resumes, Smith comes in to pitch for Los Angeles. He gives up two runs in the bottom of the ninth inning as Chicago wins, 2-1. He will be both the winning pitcher and losing pitcher in the same game.

Scorecard — Name: ____________________

Category	# Right		# of Pts.		Tot. Pts.
Great Moments - 1 Roll		x	1	=	
Great Moments - 2 Rolls		x	2	=	
Great Moments - 3 Rolls		x	3	=	
Ballparks - 1 Roll		x	1	=	
Ballparks - 2 Rolls		x	2	=	
Ballparks - 3 Rolls		x	3	=	
Hitters - 1 Roll		x	1	=	
Hitters - 2 Rolls		x	2	=	
Hitters - 3 Rolls		x	3	=	
Nicknames - 1 Roll		x	1	=	
Nicknames - 2 Rolls		x	2	=	
Nicknames - 3 Rolls		x	3	=	
Teams & Leagues - 1 Roll		x	1	=	
Teams & Leagues - 2 Rolls		x	2	=	
Teams & Leagues - 3 Rolls		x	3	=	
Pitchers - 1 Roll		x	1	=	
Pitchers - 2 Rolls		x	2	=	
Pitchers - 3 Rolls		x	3	=	
Personalities - 1 Roll		x	1	=	
Personalities - 2 Rolls		x	2	=	
Personalities - 3 Rolls		x	3	=	
Hall of Fame - 1 Roll		x	1	=	
Hall of Fame - 2 Rolls		x	2	=	
Hall of Fame - 3 Rolls		x	3	=	
World Series - 1 Roll		x	1	=	
World Series - 2 Rolls		x	2	=	
World Series - 3 Rolls		x	3	=	
Everything & Anything - 1 Roll		x	1	=	
Everything & Anything - 2 Rolls		x	2	=	
Everything & Anything - 3 Rolls		x	3	=	

Grand Total

Scorecard — Name: ____________________

Category	# Right		# of Pts.		Tot. Pts.
Great Moments - 1 Roll		x	1	=	
Great Moments - 2 Rolls		x	2	=	
Great Moments - 3 Rolls		x	3	=	
Ballparks - 1 Roll		x	1	=	
Ballparks - 2 Rolls		x	2	=	
Ballparks - 3 Rolls		x	3	=	
Hitters - 1 Roll		x	1	=	
Hitters - 2 Rolls		x	2	=	
Hitters - 3 Rolls		x	3	=	
Nicknames - 1 Roll		x	1	=	
Nicknames - 2 Rolls		x	2	=	
Nicknames - 3 Rolls		x	3	=	
Teams & Leagues - 1 Roll		x	1	=	
Teams & Leagues - 2 Rolls		x	2	=	
Teams & Leagues - 3 Rolls		x	3	=	
Pitchers - 1 Roll		x	1	=	
Pitchers - 2 Rolls		x	2	=	
Pitchers - 3 Rolls		x	3	=	
Personalities - 1 Roll		x	1	=	
Personalities - 2 Rolls		x	2	=	
Personalities - 3 Rolls		x	3	=	
Hall of Fame - 1 Roll		x	1	=	
Hall of Fame - 2 Rolls		x	2	=	
Hall of Fame - 3 Rolls		x	3	=	
World Series - 1 Roll		x	1	=	
World Series - 2 Rolls		x	2	=	
World Series - 3 Rolls		x	3	=	
Everything & Anything - 1 Roll		x	1	=	
Everything & Anything - 2 Rolls		x	2	=	
Everything & Anything - 3 Rolls		x	3	=	

Grand Total

Scorecard — Name: ____________________

Category	# Right		# of Pts.		Tot. Pts.
Great Moments - 1 Roll		x	1	=	
Great Moments - 2 Rolls		x	2	=	
Great Moments - 3 Rolls		x	3	=	
Ballparks - 1 Roll		x	1	=	
Ballparks - 2 Rolls		x	2	=	
Ballparks - 3 Rolls		x	3	=	
Hitters - 1 Roll		x	1	=	
Hitters - 2 Rolls		x	2	=	
Hitters - 3 Rolls		x	3	=	
Nicknames - 1 Roll		x	1	=	
Nicknames - 2 Rolls		x	2	=	
Nicknames - 3 Rolls		x	3	=	
Teams & Leagues - 1 Roll		x	1	=	
Teams & Leagues - 2 Rolls		x	2	=	
Teams & Leagues - 3 Rolls		x	3	=	
Pitchers - 1 Roll		x	1	=	
Pitchers - 2 Rolls		x	2	=	
Pitchers - 3 Rolls		x	3	=	
Personalities - 1 Roll		x	1	=	
Personalities - 2 Rolls		x	2	=	
Personalities - 3 Rolls		x	3	=	
Hall of Fame - 1 Roll		x	1	=	
Hall of Fame - 2 Rolls		x	2	=	
Hall of Fame - 3 Rolls		x	3	=	
World Series - 1 Roll		x	1	=	
World Series - 2 Rolls		x	2	=	
World Series - 3 Rolls		x	3	=	
Everything & Anything - 1 Roll		x	1	=	
Everything & Anything - 2 Rolls		x	2	=	
Everything & Anything - 3 Rolls		x	3	=	

Grand Total

How did you do?

500 + — King/Queen of the Throne

400-499 — Topper of the Hopper

350-399 — Porcelain Prince/Princess

300-349 — Toileterrific!

250-299 — Keep Flushing for the Stars

200-249 — Might Need a Plunger

150-199 — Gotta call the Plumber

Below 150 — Clogged

Try a different Toiletrivia Book!

Made in the USA
Middletown, DE
23 November 2019